THE JOY OF 1 JOHN 1:9

THE JOY OF 1 JOHN 1:9

D.RUTHERFORD

authorHOUSE®

AuthorHouse™ LLC
1663 Liberty Drive
Bloomington, IN 47403
www.authorhouse.com
Phone: 1-800-839-8640

Published by AuthorHouse 03/22/2014

ISBN: 978-1-4918-9918-2 (sc)
ISBN: 978-1-4918-9915-1 (e)

Library of Congress Control Number: 2014905534

Any people depicted in stock imagery provided by Thinkstock are models, and such images are being used for illustrative purposes only. Certain stock imagery © Thinkstock.

This book is printed on acid-free paper.

Because of the dynamic nature of the Internet, any web addresses or links contained in this book may have changed since publication and may no longer be valid. The views expressed in this work are solely those of the author and do not necessarily reflect the views of the publisher, and the publisher hereby disclaims any responsibility for them.

KJV
The Authorized Version or King James Version (KJV), 1611, 1769.
Outside of the United Kingdom, the KJV is in the public domain. Within the United Kingdom, the rights to the KJV are vested in the Crown.

TABLE OF CONTENTS

INTRODUCTION

Christians can greatly rejoice in 1 John 1:9 If we confess our sins, he is faithful and just to forgive us [our] sins, and to cleanse us from all unrighteousness. All biblical passages cited are from the King James Bible Version.

When we read this 1 John 1:9 verse does our joy remain full, or does it leave us feeling guilty and/ or unstable? Brothers and sisters, the New Covenant commands full Joy to every believer who reads John's message. Anyone who doesn't get the joy doesn't understand the truth of John's message, or the power of the sinless blood of Jesus Christ.

This lack of joy is due to the incorrect teaching that 1 John 1:9 means that Christians after salvation have to continually confess every sin to get God to forgive their sins. The error of claiming that Christians have to continually confess sin to God and ask for forgiveness over and over again for each time they sin, and even if they repeat the sin they were previously forgiven of grossly confuses and/ or comingles the Old Covenant of the Law with the New Covenant of Grace and fails to comprehend the power of the sinless blood of Jesus Christ.

Another misrepresentation related to this is that un-confessed sin <u>separates</u> the believer from fellowship with God, and confession is the only way to <u>restore broken fellowship</u> with God. There are huge problems with these incorrect interpretations, which is hurtful and very detrimental to those who have received salvation.

This clearly shows a failure to fully understand New Covenant confession; God's plan to gain true eternal forgiveness through His Son Jesus Christ; the similarities yet extreme differences between the Old Covenant of the Law and the New Covenant of Grace; as well as God's standard for sin.

The incorrect interpretation of 1 John 1:9 has spun off a quagmire of disinformation, and a profusion of incorrect doctrines regarding what it means to be saved.

The incorrect teaching that 1 John 1:9 also means that un-confessed sin separates Christians from God, casts doubt on the faithfulness of God. It also impugns the truthfulness of God and slanders the final finished atonement of the sinless blood of Jesus Christ. All such teaching turn people away from the free gift of salvation by the grace of God; back to the Old Covenant of the Law.

Our trust and faith must be in the Bible correctly interpreted and lived. Let us go to the New Covenant:

John 10:27 My sheep hear my voice, and I know them, and they follow me. 28 And I give unto them <u>eternal</u> life; and they shall <u>never</u> perish, <u>neither shall any [man] pluck them out of my hand.</u> 29 My Father, which gave [them] me, is greater than all; <u>and no [man] is able to pluck [them] out of my Father's hand. 30 I and [my] Father are one.</u>

The New Covenant, clearly informs us that nothing and no one shall be able to separate us from the love of God: Ro. 8: 38 For I am persuaded, that neither death, nor life, nor angels, nor principalities, nor powers, nor things present, nor things to come, 39 Nor height, nor depth, nor any other creature, shall be able to separate us from the love of God, which is in Christ Jesus our Lord.

Anyone born of God must be fully confident, convicted and persuaded by the inerrant truth of God that there is neither the power nor the hand that can take them out of or separate them from God or His love in any manner whatsoever.

The New Covenant of Grace does not support the incorrect teaching that Christians can be separated from God or His love by anyone or anything. While the whole of scripture remains relevant for God's purpose; the core of Christian faith must forever rest under the New Covenant of Grace. God forbids the mixing of Grace and Law.

Every Christian can rejoice greatly in the faithfulness of God who keeps eternally all of His children by His power. Jude informs us of God's faithfulness and power in keeping His children: Jude 1:24 Now unto him that is able to keep you from falling, and to present you faultless before the presence of his glory with exceeding joy, 25 To the only wise God our Saviour, be glory and majesty, dominion and power, both now and ever. Amen.

Redeemed From The Law

The New Covenant clearly expounds that those who have come to faith through Jesus Christ are forever redeemed from the Old Covenant of the Law and its curse:

Gal. 3:13 Christ hath redeemed us from the curse of the law, being made a curse for us: for it is written, Cursed [is] every one that hangeth on a tree: 14 That the blessing of Abraham might come on the Gentiles through Jesus Christ; that we might receive the promise of the Spirit through faith.

Gal 5:4 Christ is become of no effect unto you, whosoever of you are justified by the law; ye are fallen from grace.

1 Tim 1: 8 But we know that the law *is* good, if a man use it lawfully; 9Knowing this, that the law is not made for a righteous man, but for the lawless and disobedient, for the ungodly and for sinners, for unholy and profane, for murderers of fathers and murderers of mothers, for manslayers, 10For whoremongers, for them that defile themselves with mankind, for menstealers, for liars, for perjured persons, and if there be any other thing that is contrary to sound doctrine;11 According to the glorious gospel of the blessed God, which was committed to my trust.

We see then, that the Law is good and we use it lawfully to apply it to the aforementioned persons, and any other thing that is contrary or contradicts sound doctrine. God forbids the Law to be applied to the righteous-all whom have received salvation through Jesus Christ.

We must be confident, convicted and fully persuaded by Lord Jesus: John 6:37 All that the Father giveth me shall come to me; and him that cometh to me <u>I will in no wise cast out.</u> 38 For I came down from heaven, not to do mine own will, but the will of him that sent me. 39 And this is the Father's will which hath sent me, that of all which he hath given me <u>I should lose nothing</u>, but should raise it up again at the last day. 40 And this is the will of him that sent me, that every one which seeth the Son, and believeth on him, may have everlasting life: and I will raise him up at the last day.

Lord Jesus Christ will never cast out His people; neither will he allow anyone nor anything else to take us from Him or His love.

Dear friends, we are not only saved by salvation through grace which is the free gift, unmerited mercy and favor of God, but kept by God's power in the Son. We ought to stand in faith in believing the final, unchanging, incorruptible and everlasting truth of the Son of God.

Those who believe incorrectly that they can be separated from God and/ or lose His love cannot help but feel condemned and suffer the misery that arises out of their own misguided feelings of rejection. However, God holds all of His people eternally in His love and never separates His people from Himself, neither condemns or rejects them.

God does not want His people believing in error that He has condemned or rejected them, to the contrary He says:

Jhn 3:16 For God so loved the world, that he gave his only begotten Son, that whosoever believeth in him should not perish, but have everlasting life.17 For God sent not his Son into the world to condemn the world; but that the world through him might be saved.18 <u>He that believeth on him is not condemned</u>: but he that believeth not is condemned already, because he hath not believed in the name of the only begotten Son of God. 19 And this is the condemnation, that light is come into the world, and men loved darkness rather than light, because their deeds were evil. 20 For every one that doeth evil hateth the light, neither cometh to the light, lest his deeds should be reproved. 21 But he that doeth truth cometh to the light, that his deeds may be made manifest, that they are wrought in God.

Ro. 8:1 there *is* therefore now no condemnation to them which are in Christ Jesus, who walk not after the flesh, but after the Spirit. 2 For the law of the Spirit of life in Christ Jesus hath made me free from the law of sin and death. 3 For what the law could not do, in that it was weak through the flesh, God sending his own Son in the likeness of sinful flesh, and for sin, condemned sin in the flesh: 4 That the righteousness of the law might be fulfilled in us, who walk not after the flesh, but after the Spirit.

Christians can be confident that Jesus Christ has fully redeemed them forever from the Law of sin, curse and death, and turn fully to the Spirit of life in Christ. There are those who still think incorrectly that they can please God or be righteous through obeying the Law or some aspect of it. However, dear friends, we must trust and obey God, and not our hunches, or preferences. The Bible is undeniably clear:

God no longer accepts the Law to make people righteous with Him.

Rom. 10:4 For Christ [is] the end of the law for righteousness to every one that believeth.

Gal 2:21 I do not frustrate the grace of God: for if righteousness come by the law, then Christ is dead in vain.

Gal. 3:10 For as many as are of the works of the law are under the curse: for it is written, Cursed [is] every one that continueth not in all things which are written in the book of the law to do them. 11 But that no man is justified by the law in the sight of God it is] evident: for, the just shall live by faith.

Jesus Christ has fulfilled the law for us and as Christians God has enabled us to fulfill the law:

Ro. 13: 8 Owe no man anything, but to love one another: for he that loves another has fulfilled the law. 9 For this, You shall not commit adultery, You shall not kill, You shall not steal, You shall not bear false witness, You shall not covet; and if there be any other commandment, it is briefly comprehended in this saying, namely, You shall love your neighbor as yourself: 10 Love works no ill to his neighbor: therefore love is the fulfilling of the law.

Some who have read my beginning statements may experience discomfort and/or might think that I am saying Christians can not only live in sin, but also feel free to continue in it as though it is nothing to God. I want to assure you I am saying no such things. What I pray through God's inerrant word, correctly interpreted is to show the truth of salvation and what God commands Christians to do regarding sin, in the way that honors God according to His word, not unbiblical teaching.

I also pray to help Christians gain the full understanding of biblical New Covenant forgiveness through the sinless blood of Lord Jesus Christ. This is necessary because the forgiveness of the Old and New Covenants are absolutely not the same. We must look at the two Covenants to gain the full understanding through God of His purpose and function of them for all mankind; as well as how they are alike, and yet differ greatly from one another. God forbids absolutely the blending or comingling of these two separate Covenants. Yet we find this is often done by some in error.

If we are truly Christians, we will do God's will and it will be proven in believing the whole Gospel message and in our daily walk because we are empowered and indwelt by the Holy Spirit. I pray that all Christians will continually grow and be established in grace, and this we will do by the faith of Jesus Christ.

THE TWO COVENANTS

Again, it is clear that the misinterpretation 1 John 1: 9 is due in part to failure to understand both the Old Covenant of the Law and the New Covenant. These two separate Covenants are similar in that each was ordained by God. Under each covenant penitent sinners are commanded by God to confess their sin to the high priest/mediator who is ordained and commanded to offer sacrifice to God to obtain forgiveness for penitent sinners, in order for them to avoid the penalty imposed per each covenant; as well as to receive their respective blessings.

God ordained the high priests of each covenant as the only ones appointed to offer unblemished blood sacrifice to make atonement to obtain forgiveness for the sins of all of the penitent sinners as a whole. God also ordained each of the high priests of the covenants to serve as mediators between the people and God, and to oversee each respective Covenant, their order, proper function and service of the priests under them.

The high priest in his role of mediator is one whom God appoints to intervene between two, (men and God) either in order to make or restore peace and friendship, or form a compact, or for ratifying a covenant. The mediator also acts as a medium of communication, arbitrator.

THE OLD COVENANT OF THE LAW

God demanded the whole Old Covenant of the Law to be obeyed without exception. He did not give anyone the option or authority to pick out and obey only the laws that they liked. The people certainly loved God, but also obeyed because the penalty for sin under the Law is the curse and death.

The Bible confirms from the Old Testament to the New Testament that the whole law must be obeyed.

Deu. 27:26 Cursed [be] he that confirmeth not [all] the words of this law to do them. And all the people shall say, Amen.

Jam. 2:10 For whosoever shall keep the whole law, and yet offend in one [point], he is guilty of all.

Throughout the year when the penitent sinners confessed their sins to God, they well understood that forgiveness could only be obtained if it were also accompanied by the priests offering of a sacrifice to make atonement. No sin was too small or could be overlooked. Even if the people sinned ignorantly they were still considered guilty. The people were guilty even if they committed sins of omission, as well as overt or covert sins. The people were also considered guilty if they knew of someone else's sin and kept it hidden. The people could along with their own sin, confess those of their fathers and their nation.

Although there was a yearly sacrifice of atonement for the people as a whole, God still required that each of the people confess their sins throughout the year as soon as it came to their knowledge or they understood that they had committed a sin and offer the appropriate atonement through the priests to gain God's forgiveness. Let us keep in mind as mentioned earlier that the people were highly motivated to confess sin out of love for God as well as to avoid the penalty of the Law. For this cause we can well understand the necessity of their keeping short accounts as unconfessed sin could bring severe punishment.

Under the Old Covenant of the law, we can clearly understand the pattern established and commanded by God; that there could be no forgiveness of sins without its accompanying sacrifice of atonement through the priests. *In other words the penitent sinners' confession alone although required was insufficient to obtain forgiveness under the Law,* Under the Law it is also important to understand that some sins led to punishment for which no forgiveness could be obtained.

Under the Law God required that a yearly atonement be made by the high priest each year:

Leviticus 16: 33 And he shall make an atonement for the holy sanctuary, and he shall make an atonement for the tabernacle of the congregation, and for the altar, and he shall make an atonement for the priests, and for all the people of the congregation. 34 And this shall be an everlasting statute unto you, to make atonement for the children of Israel for all their sins once a year. And he did as the Lord commanded Moses.

All of the daily confession and sacrifices of the penitents and all The Old Covenant priests could only gain a temporary forgiveness of the people. Even the yearly sacrifice made by the high priest to make atonement to gain forgiveness for the sins of all the people as a whole lasted only a year. This is because when Adam sinned, sin and death entered the world into all flesh. Therefore the blood of the unblemished sacrificed animals once shed, would decay and vanish away into corruption over time and could never be re-used.

So we can clearly see the weakness of all their sacrifices to understand that the forgiveness or pardon under the Old Covenant could only gain a temporary reprieve for a limited time, which came as it were with an expiration date. For this reason God commanded a yearly fresh sacrifice on behalf of all the people as a whole, as well as for subsequent sins of individuals throughout the year. We can fully understand that the priest's work was never done. We understand that all of these sacrifices under the Law were powerless to take away any sin permanently, but allowed the sinner to escape death, to live and be restored to the approval and fellowship with God—only until the next sin.

Although God commanded each year that the high priest/mediator alone make confession and sacrifice of atonement for the people, he first had to confess his own personal sins and the sins of his household, including the priests under him. Only after this could he confess the sins of the people and make sacrifice of atonement to gain forgiveness from God for the sins of the people as a whole.

The high priest/mediator was commanded by God to sacrifice certain always perfectly unblemished animals. He would take two of these animals from among and in behalf of the people. He would cast a lot to see which would be taken as a sin offering. The remaining animal would always be left alive for the high priest/mediator to confess all the sins of the people upon its head. This live animal is called the scapegoat, which then would be sent away, out of the camp into an uninhabited region carrying all the sins of the people with it. Under the Old Covenant we can clearly see the mercy of God in that He allowed animals to be sacrificed as a substitute for man; instead of requiring the death of every man that sinned. Nevertheless, as one Old Covenant high priest died, another had to be ordained to take his place.

Once again it is vital to understand that <u>none</u> of the sacrifices of atonement gained permanent forgiveness to the penitent sinner from God under the Old Covenant of the Law, and *even the high priest/ mediator had to confess his own personal sins, and that of his house, to make an atonement for himself <u>first</u> <u>before</u> he could confess the sins of the people and make sacrifice of atonement for the people as a whole, to gain God's forgiveness.*

GOD'S PURPOSE OF THE LAW EXPLAINED IN THE NEW COVENANT:

The Old Covenant of the Law is of external worship and commands written on tablets of stone. It was given by God through the Law of Moses, and enforced by curses and death. The Law is good, although very severe. It demonstrates God's mercy as through it He had a wonderful purpose that the law served as a school teacher, and to teach people they are sinners in need of a Saviour and to prepare them to receive the gospel message. Therefore God concluded all under sin so that at the coming of Jesus Christ the Messiah whosoever would believe on Him will be saved.

Gal. 3: 19 Wherefore then [serveth] the law? It was added because of transgressions, till the seed should come to whom the promise was made; [and it was] ordained by angels in the hand of a mediator. 20 Now a mediator is not [a mediator] of one, but God is one. 21 [Is] the law then against the promises of God? <u>God forbid: for if there had been a law given which could have given life, verily righteousness should have been by the law.</u> <u>22 But the scripture hath concluded all under sin, that the promise by faith of Jesus Christ might be given to them that believe.</u> 23 But before faith came, we were kept under the law, shut up unto the faith which should afterwards be revealed. 24 Wherefore the law was our schoolmaster [to bring us] unto Christ, that we might be justified by faith. <u>25But after that faith is come, we are no longer under a schoolmaster.</u>

We leave the Old Covenant of the Law having grasped its understanding, and God's purpose and function of it to obtain forgiveness for the people as a whole. Again we can conclude that between confession of sin to God and forgiveness by God there always has to be a high priest; who acts as a mediator between man and God; ordained and appointed by God. This high priest/mediator alone is commanded and ordained by God, to offer the perfect unblemished blood sacrifice for the people as a whole, to gain forgiveness and make reconciliation between them and God. Again, *it is vital to understand that while the confession of sin was required, of itself and without the high priest/mediator/giving of atoning unblemished blood sacrifice, God absolutely did not accept the confession nor give any forgiveness of sins whatsoever to any sinner.*

This then is the non-negotiable pattern that God commanded, ordained and established. <u>Both the Old and New Covenants follow this absolute pattern.</u> However it is in understanding these two covenants that we clearly see how they compare yet find that they greatly differ from one another.

THE MESSIANIC PROMISE

All the prophets proclaimed and declared that the Messiah was to come and is in fact Jesus Christ the Son of God. Acts 10: 36 The word which God sent unto the children of Israel, preaching peace by Jesus Christ: (he is Lord of all:) 37 That word, I say, ye know, which was published throughout all Judaea, and began from Galilee, after the baptism which John preached; 38 How God anointed Jesus of Nazareth with the Holy Ghost and with power: who went about doing good, and healing all that were oppressed of the devil; for God was with him. 39 And we are witnesses of all things which he did both in the land of the Jews, and in Jerusalem; whom they slew and hanged on a tree: 40 Him God raised up the third day, and shewed him openly; 41 Not to all the people, but unto witnesses chosen before God, even to us, who did eat and drink with him after he rose from the dead. 42 And he commanded us to preach unto the people, and to testify that it is he which was ordained of God to be the Judge of quick and dead. <u>43 To him give all the prophets witness, that through his name whosoever believeth in him shall receive remission of sins.</u>

Remission is the release from the bondage or imprisonment of sin.

It is also the forgiveness or pardon, of sins (letting them go as if they had never been committed), and the remission of the penalty of sins.

The Messiah or Saviour God promised would be so powerful, that He would forever take away or purge completely all the sins of all who believe in Him. Furthermore His salvation would not be limited to the nation of Israel, but would be for all peoples, who would believe in Him. The Bible declares of Jesus Christ the Son of God:

Jhn 1:29 The next day John seeth Jesus coming unto him, and saith, Behold the Lamb of God, which taketh away the sin of the world.

1 Peter 1: 17 And if ye call on the Father, who without respect of persons judgeth according to every man's work, pass the time of your sojourning [here] in fear: 18 Forasmuch as ye know that ye were not redeemed with corruptible things, [as] silver and gold, from your vain conversation [received] by tradition from your fathers; <u>19 But with the precious blood of Christ, as of a lamb without blemish and without spot: 20 Who verily was foreordained before the foundation of the world,</u> but was manifest in these last times for you, 21 Who by him do believe in God, that raised him up from the dead, and gave him glory; that your faith and hope might be in God.

Understanding
The New Covenant

The New Covenant is ordained by God. It is the absolute non-negotiable, uncompromising, final, finished, incorruptible standard and completion of the Bible for all time through Jesus Christ the risen Saviour and Son of God. There are no "plan B's, multiple choices, or alternatives to the New Covenant. God has ordained the whole New Covenant commands to be obeyed without exception. God does not grant anyone the option to pick out only the parts of the New Covenant that they like. The Bible clearly states God's penalty without exception for all those who refuse to believe or reject His son Jesus Christ.

Rev. 21:8 But the fearful, and unbelieving, and the abominable, and murderers, and whoremongers, and sorcerers, and idolaters, and all liars, shall have their part in the lake which burneth with fire and brimstone: which is the second death.

Mat 25:41Then shall he say also unto them on the left hand, Depart from me, ye cursed, into everlasting fire, prepared for the devil and his angels:

The New Covenant was promised by God Himself, to Abraham and his seed <u>before God brought the Old Covenant of the Law into effect.</u> God confirms the New Covenant in both the Old and New Testament:

Gen. 17:5 Neither shall thy name any more be called Abram, but thy name shall be Abraham; for a father of many nations have I made thee. 6 And I will make thee exceeding fruitful, and I will make nations of thee, and kings shall come out of thee. 7 And I will establish my covenant between me and thee and thy seed after thee in their generations for an everlasting covenant, to be a God unto thee, and to thy seed after thee.

Gal 3:16 Now to Abraham and his seed were the promises made. He saith not, And to seeds, as of many; but as of one, And to thy seed which is Christ. 17 And this I say, that the covenant, that was confirmed before of God in Christ, the law, which was four hundred and thirty years after, cannot disannul, that it should make the promise of none effect. Disannul: G288 meaning-akyroō, to make of non-effect; invalidate.

God promised in the Old Covenant that he would make a New Covenant. God promised that this New Covenant would be an everlasting Covenant for all eternity. God promised that His New Covenant would disannul the weak ineffective Old Covenant Law, its priesthood, and ineffectual sacrifices.

The Bible absolutely confirms that the Old Covenant Law which came after God's promise to Abraham and his seed has no power to neither terminate nor invalidate the New Covenant in any manner whatsoever.

God promised that this New Covenant would be so effectual through His Son Jesus Christ, that not only would He take away all sins, but that God would remember them no more.

Jesus is the Son of God. Jesus is God, and He was always with God His Father. Jesus is fully and completely man and God having no beginning and no end, just as God the Father. Jesus is the co-creator of heaven and earth. Jesus Christ is the second Person of the Godhead: God the Father, God the Son, God the Holy Spirit. God declares of His Son: Heb. 1: 1 God, who at sundry times and in divers manners spake in time past unto the fathers by the prophets, 2 Hath in these last days spoken unto us by his Son, whom he hath appointed heir of all things, by whom also he made the worlds;

3 Who being the brightness of his glory, and the express image of his person, and upholding all things by the word of his power, when he had by himself purged our sins, sat down on the right hand of the Majesty on high: 4 Being made so much better than the angels, as he hath by inheritance obtained a more excellent name than they. 5 For unto which of the angels said he at any time, Thou art my Son, this day have I begotten thee? And again, I will be to him a Father, and he shall be to me a Son? 6 And again, when he bringeth in the firstbegotten into the world, he saith, And let all the angels of God worship him. 7 And of the angels he saith, Who maketh his angels spirits, and his ministers a flame of fire. 8 But unto the Son he saith, Thy throne, O God, is for ever and ever: a sceptre of righteousness is the sceptre of thy kingdom. 9 Thou hast loved righteousness, and hated iniquity; therefore God, even thy God, hath anointed thee with the oil of gladness above thy fellows. 10 And, Thou, Lord, in the beginning hast laid the foundation of the earth; and the heavens are the works of thine hands: 11 They shall perish; but thou remainest; and they all shall wax old as doth a garment; 12 And as a vesture shalt thou fold them up, and they shall be changed: but thou art the same, and thy years shall not fail.

Jesus Christ was born to the virgin Mary. Jesus Christ was conceived of the virgin Mary through the Holy Spirit. His birth was prophesied hundreds of years in the Bible before it came to pass:

Isa 7:14 Therefore the Lord himself shall give you a sign; Behold, a virgin shall conceive, and bear a son, and shall call his name Immanuel.

Isa 9: 6 For unto us a child is born, unto us a son is given: and the government shall be upon his shoulder: and his name shall be called Wonderful, Counsellor, The mighty God, The everlasting Father, and The Prince of Peace. 7 Of the increase of his government and peace there shall be no end, upon the throne of David, and upon his kingdom, to order it, and to establish it with judgment and with justice from henceforth even for ever. The zeal of the Lord of hosts will perform this.

God affirmed to Joseph espoused to the virgin Mary the full and true nature of her pregnancy to dispel Joseph's doubts, as he found her to be pregnant before his consummation with her: Mat 1:20 But while he thought on these things, behold, the angel of the Lord appeared unto him in a dream, saying, Joseph, thou son of David, fear not to take unto thee Mary thy wife: for that which is conceived in her is of the Holy Ghost. 21 And she shall bring forth a son, and thou shalt call his name JESUS: for he shall save his people from their sins. 22 Now all this was done, that it might be fulfilled which was spoken of the Lord by the prophet, saying, 23 Behold, a virgin shall be with child, and shall bring forth a son, and they shall call his name Emmanuel, which being interpreted is, God with us. 24 Then Joseph being raised from sleep did as the angel of the Lord had bidden him, and took unto him his wife: 25 And knew her not till she had brought forth her firstborn son: and he called his name JESUS.

Jesus in His earthly ministry preached the gospel message of good news. Jesus Christ confirmed that He is the Messiah. Jesus Christ is the Testator of the New Covenant and established the Lord's Supper as a memoriam to His final finished and complete work on the cross, for all who believe on His name.

Jesus Christ loved family, friends, devoted apostles, disciples and all men, even His enemies. Yet, Jesus suffered hunger, thirst, temptation, homelessness, betrayal, denial, and the continual hatred, jealousy, harassment of the wicked and their ceaseless death threats. He suffered rejection mockery, and humiliation from those whom He came to save. The religious establishment of His day in vain even put Him to death on the cross in hopes of keeping their position of power by silencing His gospel. Nevertheless He lived a perfect sinless life. Jesus Christ is the first and only sinless human being who ever lived. Jesus Christ never sinned, and never had any sin whatsoever.

The New Covenant came into effect upon the death of Jesus Christ. Jesus came to the earth to die for the sins of mankind. He gave His life freely for us. No one took it from Him. He gave it up freely as a sinless sacrifice for our sins. Jesus is the Son of God; no one had the power to take His life He gave it up freely: Jhn 10:14 I am the good shepherd, and know my sheep, and am known of mine. 15 As the Father knoweth me, even so know I the Father: and I lay down my life for the sheep.16 And other sheep I have, which are not of this fold: them also I must bring, and they shall hear my voice; and there shall be one fold, and one shepherd.17 Therefore doth my Father love me, because I lay down my life, that I might take it again. <u>18 No man taketh it from me, but I lay it down of myself. I have power to lay it down, and I have power to take it again. This commandment have I received of my Father.</u>

The Bible says the penalty of sin is the curse and death and that we all have sinned. Under the Old Testament Law of Moses God allowed an animal to be sacrificed for the sins of a limited group of persons—the nation Israel. However, under the New Testament Jesus Christ became the perfect sinless sacrifice to take away the sins of <u>all</u> of mankind on the cross.

It is error to think that Christ's death on the cross automatically saves all people. The biblical truth is that Christ's death means all who confess and believe on Christ, as Saviour will be saved and have eternal life through Christ. See John 3:16-21.

THE PERMANENT HIGH PRIEST/ MEDIATOR OF THE NEW COVENANT

1Ti 2:5 For there is one God, and one mediator between God and men, the man Christ Jesus;

Hbr 9:15 And for this cause he is the mediator of the new testament, that by means of death, for the redemption of the transgressions that were under the first testament, they which are called might receive the promise of eternal inheritance.

Because Jesus Christ met all of God's requirements in offering the perfect sinless sacrifice of Himself; God has appointed His Son Jesus Christ to be the sole High Priest/Mediator between God and men, for all eternity.

Heb. 7: 19 For the law made nothing perfect, but the bringing in of a better hope did; by the which we draw nigh unto God. 20 And inasmuch as not without an oath he was made priest:21 (For those priests were made without an oath; but this with an oath by him that said unto him, The Lord sware and will not repent, Thou art a priest for ever after the order of Melchisedec:) 22 By so much was Jesus made a surety of a better testament.23 And they truly were many priests, because they were not suffered to continue by reason of death:24 But this man, because he continueth ever, hath an unchangeable priesthood. 25 Wherefore he is able also to save them to the uttermost that come unto God by him, seeing he ever liveth to make intercession for them. 26 For such an high priest became us, who is holy, harmless, undefiled, separate from sinners, and made higher than the heavens; <u>27 Who needeth not daily, as those high priests, to offer up sacrifice, first for his own sins, and then for the people's: for this he did once, when he offered up himself.</u> 28 For the law maketh men high priests which have infirmity; but the word of the oath, which was since the law, maketh the Son, who is consecrated for evermore.

Furthermore God appointed Lord Jesus Christ as the Head of the church; He guards it, establishes its order and oversees the proper function and service of the priests under Him. Unlike the sinful high priest/priests of the Old Covenant of the Law, Jesus Christ never had to confess His own sin, because He never had any sin. Of Jesus Christ the scriptures declares:

2Cr 5:21 For he hath made him to be sin for us, who knew no sin; that we might be made the righteousness of God in him.

1Pe 2:22 Who did no sin, neither was guile found in his mouth:

1Jo 3:5 And ye know that he was manifested to take away our sins; and in him is no sin

No one can come to Jesus Christ the Son of God unless God the Father first draws them. Jesus Christ declares: Jhn. 6:44 No man can come to me, <u>except the Father which hath sent me draw him</u>: and I will raise him up at the last day.

Jhn 3:16 For God so loved the world, that he gave his only begotten Son, that whosoever believeth in him should not perish, but have everlasting life.

Penitent Sinners
And The New Covenant

Under the New Covenant, God commands that all penitent sinners without exception come and confess to His Son Jesus Christ, whom He sent into the world and has appointed the eternal and everlasting High Priest/Mediator over the house of God and the Head of the church. God sent Jesus Christ alone as Saviour to save people from their sins.

Again because Jesus Christ is the ordained High Priest/Mediator alone, God commands that all penitent sinners make their confession to Jesus Christ alone. Jesus Christ the Son of God is the only way to enter into the kingdom of God the Father.

Jhn 14:6 Jesus saith unto him, I am the way, the truth, and the life: <u>no man cometh unto the Father, but by me.</u>

2Pe. 3:9 The Lord is not slack concerning his promise, as some men count slackness; but is longsuffering to us-ward, not willing that any should perish, but that all should come to repentance.

Under the New Covenant while the penitent sinners' confession is required; it is the High Priest/Mediator Jesus Christ's imputing of His unblemished sinless atoning blood sacrifice which begins, and finishes it and gains eternal forgiveness from God. This forgiveness is permanent from God, and is never diminished in any way. It remains forever given to those who have been redeemed.

The Bible declares: Ro. 10:10 The word is nigh thee, [even] in thy mouth, and in thy heart: that is, the word of faith, which we preach; 9That if thou shalt confess with thy mouth the Lord Jesus, and shalt believe in thine heart that God hath raised him from the dead, thou shalt be saved. 10For with the heart man believeth unto righteousness; and with the mouth confession is made unto salvation. 11For the scripture saith, Whosoever believeth on him shall not be ashamed. 12For there is no difference between the Jew and the Greek: for the same Lord over all is rich unto all that call upon him. 13For whosoever shall call upon the name of the Lord shall be saved.

We clearly understand our confession is made to the High Priest/ Mediator of the New Covenant, not the disannulled Old Covenant High Priest of the Law. *We gain the understanding that our confession does not mean to ask God for forgiveness over and over again for our sins, like the penitent sinners of the Old Covenant of the Law.* New Covenant confession means to turn from sin to God; to fully agree to a covenant: Confess: G3670 homologeō, meaning: to assent, i.e. covenant, acknowledge:— con (pro) fess, confession is made, give thanks, promise.

This confession (G3470) unto salvation even, after salvation, is held fast as finished. Some call it the credo, or creed, but simply put it is the expected, faithful, consistent confession and stance of the whole church and each saint individually, lived out in word and deed, to be practiced in everyday life. This confession is steadfast and upholds the complete finished, final New Covenant message of the finished, final complete for all time work of Christ, forever. This stance is in complete love, faith, confidence, assurance of the inerrancy of the work and word of God, affirming Jesus Christ at every level and against all contradictions. It is accomplished through the indwelling of the Holy Spirit.

Furthermore the whole church consistently affirms that God alone is the absolute, final, sole, eternal way, truth, light, standard, and authority, for all men, for all time. He is the Source and Sovereign of All life, and every soul shall give account to Him.

Heb. 4:14 Seeing then that we have a great high priest, that is passed into the heavens, Jesus the Son of God, let us hold fast our profession.

Heb. 10:23 let us hold fast the profession of our faith without wavering, (for he is faithful that promised). This profession that we hold fast is G3671 homologia, from the same as in G3670. To hold fast means G2722 Katecho, to hold down fast, (lit. or fig.)—have, hold (fast), keep (in memory), possess, retain, seize, and stay. This is a one-time permanent confession we must make to God, who offers a one-time atonement-the sinless blood sacrifice of His Son Lord Jesus Christ.

Christ's forgiveness is complete, permanent, final and finished, once for all. His forgiveness is the eternal termination of the wrath of God against sin; it is the eternal release from the guilt of sin which oppresses the conscience, and the eternal remission of the punishment of sin, which is eternal death. Dearly beloved God is not angry with you or any of His people ever again because of Jesus Christ.

In his justification of all believers, then, all our sins past present and future are forgiven permanently; and the guilt and punishment thereof permanently removed: Acts 13:38 Be it known unto you therefore, men and brethren, that through this man is preached unto you the forgiveness of sins: 39 And by him all that believe are justified from all things, from which ye could not be justified by the law of Moses.

God sees the believer as without sin and guilt in Christ: Rom. 8:33 Who shall lay any thing to the charge of God's elect? It is God that justifieth. 34 Who is he that condemneth? It is Christ that died, yea rather, that is risen again, who is even at the right hand of God, who also maketh intercession for us.

His righteousness is unto all and upon all them that believe (Rom. 3:22-28) see Ro, 5: 17-21; 1 Cor. 1:30.

Once sinners confess and repent of their sins believing in the name of Jesus Christ who imputes His righteousness to them—all their sins are forgiven by God the Father, once for all and they receive the indwelling gift of the Holy Spirit. Lord Jesus' imputing of the one-time offering of His sinless atoning sacrifice is completely sufficient for taking and washing away all of our sins. <u>He has nothing else to offer because there is absolutely nothing else to offer, or can be offered other than His one sacrifice.</u> His one offering for sin is absolutely finished and final. He is not like those sinful old high priests under the annulled Mosaic Law, whose work was never finished because they could not obtain permanent forgiveness for the people.

God absolutely forbids adding anything to His Son's sinless sacrifice or taking anything away from it which rejects its eternal absolute truthfulness. Any additional works to obtain forgiveness after salvation is received, is in actual fact rejecting the significance of Christ's shed blood on the cross, death, burial and resurrection and spurning the Holy Spirit's work. It is error to teach that Christ's sacrifice still leaves you incomplete or that something else is needed to make you acceptable to God. When we believe in Christ, he makes us complete not any method to gain salvation through good deeds or any further works to be right with God:

Col. 2: 8 Beware lest any man spoil you through philosophy and vain deceit, after the tradition of men, after the rudiments of the world, and not after Christ.9 For in him dwelleth all the fulness of the Godhead bodily.10 And ye are complete in him, which is the head of all principality and power:11 In whom also ye are circumcised with the circumcision made without hands, in putting off the body of the sins of the flesh by the circumcision of Christ:12 Buried with him in baptism, wherein also ye are risen with him through the faith of the operation of God, who hath raised him from the dead.13 And you, being dead in your sins and the uncircumcision of your flesh, hath he quickened together with him, having forgiven you all trespasses; 14 Blotting out the handwriting of ordinances that was against us, which was contrary to us, and took it out of the way, nailing it to his cross;15 And having spoiled principalities and powers, he made a shew of them openly, triumphing over them in it.

Our loving relationship leads us to follow him in willing obedience and service. It is essential to understand absolutely that we cannot be saved by our good deeds, or obtain further forgiveness after salvation is received. However all who are saved will produce good fruit or works through the indwelling Holy Spirit. Please note what the Bible says: Eph. 2:8-9: For by grace are ye saved through faith; and that not of yourselves: it is the gift of God: 9 Not of works, lest any man should boast. This does not mean that the Christian does not have any works, but both their source and the ability to carry them out is through the empowerment of the Holy Spirit.

As new creatures, in Christ Jesus, indwelt by the Holy Spirit, we fully understand that it is the power of God that enables us to be obedient to God. Without Jesus we can do nothing at all, for He declares: 5 I am the vine, ye are the branches: He that abideth in me, and I in him, the same bringeth forth much fruit: for without me ye can do nothing.

All of our sins past present and future are completely cleansed away; God keeps no account, remembrance, or imputation of sin to all who have received grace.

Through Jesus Christ, we are given peace and reconciliation with God. God now regards those who are saved as His children apart of His family and kingdom for all eternity. The penitent sinner is now called a saint: (G40 hagios) phys. pure, mor. blameless or religious, consecrated-most holy (one, thing), saint. This is the child of God, through Jesus Christ made a new creature, with a new Master (God), new name, a new nature, empowered by the Holy Spirit to live above the old man or old nature. He or she is now born again of the Holy Spirit. This then is salvation the free un-merited gift of grace through Jesus Christ the Son of God.

Without the perfect sinless sacrifice of the shed blood, bodily death on the cross, burial, resurrection and ascension of Jesus Christ we still would be under the penalty of our sins under the Law of the Old

Covenant of the Law subject to the penalty of it, and without hope in the world. Thanks to God who has saved us for all eternity.

Rom 4:6 Even as David also describeth the blessedness of the man, unto whom God imputeth righteousness without works, 7 Saying, Blessed are they whose iniquities are forgiven, and whose sins are covered. <u>8 Blessed is the man to whom the Lord will not impute sin.</u>

Heb. 10:16 This is the covenant that I will make with them after those days, saith the Lord, I will put my laws into their hearts, and in their minds will I write them; <u>17 And their sins and iniquities will</u> I remember no more. 18 Now where remission of these is, there is no more offering for sin.

Let us examine more closely the meaning of no more as found in Heb.10:17-18: No more means: i.e. G3756 (ou) and G3661 (me); a double negative strengthening the denial; not at all:—any more, at all, not by any (no) means, neither, never, no (at all), in no case (wise), nor ever, not (at all, in any wise).

Let us now note these verses in their fullest sense: Heb.10: 17 and their sins and iniquities will I remember absolutely not at all, any more, at all by any (no means, neither, never, no (at all), in no case (wise), nor ever, not (at all, in any wise). Heb.10: 18 reads in this same way.

We can easily see the awesome nature of the Atonement in Jesus Christ alone. Not only are we forgiven for all eternity, but it is crystal clear from the above passages, not only has He taken our sins away, but also keeps absolutely no record or any account of them any longer. This is not a license to sin but freedom to exalt God first in everything, and eagerly do His will out of sheer love and gratitude for what He has done for us.

No more offering for sin this cannot be said often enough when we confess our sins to Jesus Christ He imputes His sinless blood sacrifice to us. Christ's sinless sacrifice has completely met <u>all</u> of God's requirements, and made further sacrifices of atonement for sin <u>forever un-necessary</u>. Through Jesus Christ alone who is the perfect, sinless sacrifice of atonement, all who believe receive forever the complete permanent forgiveness of God for all eternity.

(Atonement—meaning: G1242-diathēkē: in the NT the restoration of the favor of God to sinners that repent and put their trust in the expiatory death of Christ.

Christians are kept by the power of God who will not suffer any of them to be lost: Heb. 10:38 the just shall live by faith: but if any man draw back, my soul shall have no pleasure in him. 39 <u>But we are not of them who draw back unto perdition; but of them that believe to the saving of the soul.</u>

1 Pe. 1:3 Blessed be the God and Father of our Lord Jesus Christ, which according to his abundant mercy hath begotten us again unto a lively hope by the resurrection of Jesus Christ from the dead, 4 To an inheritance incorruptible, and undefiled, and that fadeth not away, reserved in heaven for you, <u>5 Who are kept by the power of God through faith unto salvation ready to be revealed in the last time.</u>

Jud 1:24 Now unto him that is able to keep you from falling, and to present you faultless before the presence of his glory with exceeding joy,

25 To the only wise God our Saviour, be glory and majesty, dominion and power, both now and ever.

We must keep before us the eternal efficacy of the blood of Jesus Christ. The blood of Christ because it is perfectly sinless, is incorruptible, and impossible for it to rot, decay or vanish away into corruption. Therefore the Sinless blood of Jesus Christ remains the eternally effective sinless sacrifice that completely washes away all sins to bring salvation to all who believe on Him. <u>This is why it was only necessary for Christ to have offered His sinless Blood only once.</u> The sinless blood of Jesus Christ retains its efficacy for all eternity for those who have been washed in it from all their sins. See Hebrews chapters 9 in which the blood of Jesus Christ's sinless sacrifice is contrasted with the blood of animal sacrifices; showing the superiority and eternal efficacy of the blood of Jesus Christ. Also see chapter 10 of Hebrews.

It is common for some to think in error that there are many roads that lead to salvation and that it is not necessary to come through Jesus Christ. However, the inerrant word of God tells us the eternal truth:

John 14:6 Jesus saith unto him, I am the way, the truth, and the life: no man cometh unto the Father, but by me.

Now if anyone persists in trying to enter into heaven other than through Jesus Christ, He says: John 10:1 Verily, verily, I say unto you, He that entereth not by the door into the sheepfold, but climbeth up some other way, the same is a thief and a robber.

Jhn 10:9 I am the door: by me if any man enter in, he shall be saved, and shall go in and out, and find pasture.

As mentioned earlier, God gives no forgiveness for all eternity to those who reject His Son Jesus Christ:

Hbr 10:26 For if we sin wilfully after that we have received the knowledge of the truth, there remaineth no more sacrifice for sins, 27 But a certain fearful looking for of judgment and fiery indignation, which shall devour the adversaries. 28 He that despised Moses' law died without mercy under two or three witnesses: 29 Of how much sorer punishment, suppose ye, shall he be thought worthy, who hath trodden under foot the Son of God, and hath counted the blood of the covenant, wherewith he was sanctified, an unholy thing, and hath done despite unto the Spirit of grace? 30 For we know him that hath said, Vengeance belongeth unto me, I will recompense, saith the Lord. And again, The Lord shall judge his people. 31 It is a fearful thing to fall into the hands of the living God'

Sin After Salvation

No doubt some believers ponder that since the sinless blood of Jesus Christ purges us from all sins, giving complete forgiveness eternally; God never remembering them nor putting it on our record; i.e. no longer imputing them to us anymore; which makes it un-necessary for us to keep confessing and asking for forgiveness of sins over and over again—then why does the New Covenant give examples of Christians who sin after salvation?

The answer is that while it is true that the New Covenant cites examples of Christians who sin after salvation; nevertheless God neither imputes nor remembers their sins at all anymore. Neither do they lose their salvation; they remain eternally forgiven. This remains absolutely eternally true for all Christians.

It is essential to keep in mind and understand that God alone has set the final, complete and eternal standard for imputing sin. All who have been saved through Jesus Christ have died, i.e. been delivered from the Law of sin and death; therefore: Rom 5:13 (For until the law sin was in the world: but sin is not imputed when there is no law. The issue of God's forgiveness via atonement through Jesus for all believers is once and for all settled for all eternity, it is finished. God has not left us on our own, nor are we "saved sinners". The penitent sinner is not just forgiven, and left to flounder alone. Nor is he or she an old man dusted off and cleaned up outwardly with a somewhat improved old nature, No, no he or she is regenerated, made a completely new creature, indwelt by God the Father, God the Son, and God the Holy Spirit made a child of the Living God.

God tells us over and over in a multitude of ways throughout His word that Christians are not given a license to sin, but made free from the bondage of sin to serve God and one another in love, and gratitude for what God's Son has done for us.

The Gospel message leaves no wiggle room for anyone claiming to be a Christian while practicing a life of habitual sinning. One who is truly born of God does not live a life of habitual sinning.

This might be shocking to some; nevertheless, the truth is that Christians do not have to choose to practice any sin. Through salvation every believer is dead to sin and alive to Christ:

Ro. 6: 3 Know ye not, that so many of us as were baptized into Jesus Christ were baptized into his death: 4 Therefore we are buried with him by baptism into death: that like as Christ was raised up from the dead by the glory of the Father, even so we also should walk in newness of life. 5 For if we have been planted together in the likeness of his death, we shall be also [in the likeness] of [his] resurrection. 6 Knowing this, that our old man is crucified with [him], that the body of sin might be destroyed, that henceforth we should not serve sin. 7 For he that is dead is freed from sin.

Through faith in Jesus Christ the power and dominion of sin is broken in the lives of Christians. Under the New Covenant Christians are commanded, and enabled to overcome sin:

Ro. 6: 13 Neither yield ye your members [as] instruments of unrighteousness unto sin: but yield yourselves unto God, as those that are alive from the dead, and your members [as] instruments of righteousness unto God. 14 For sin shall not have dominion over you: for ye are not under the law, but under grace. 15 What then? shall we sin, because we are not under the law, but under grace? God forbid. 16 Know ye not, that to whom ye yield yourselves servants to obey, his servants ye are to whom ye obey; whether of sin unto death, or of obedience unto righteousness? 17 But God be thanked, that ye were the servants of sin, but ye have obeyed from the heart that form of doctrine which was delivered you. 18 Being then made free from sin, ye became the servants of righteousness.

It is through the correct understanding of God's word that we learn clearly how to live holy lives, and the power God has given us, through the Holy Spirit, to overcome sin.

Christ empowers and commands us to "crucify the flesh with its affections and lusts". God forbids us to believe or see any temptation to sin as somehow "extraordinary" or so unusual as to require some kind of special treatment or understanding when God says in His word:

1Cor.10: 13 There hath no temptation taken you but such as is <u>common to man</u>: but God *is* faithful, who will not suffer you to be tempted above that ye are able; but will with the temptation also make a way to escape, that ye may be able to bear *it*. 14 Wherefore, my dearly beloved, flee from idolatry.

Again God's word tells us: Heb. 12:1 Wherefore seeing we also are compassed about with so great a cloud of witnesses, let us lay aside every weight, and the sin which doth so easily beset us, and let us run with patience the race that is set before us, 2Looking unto Jesus the author and finisher of [our] faith; who for the joy that was set before him endured the cross, despising the shame, and is set down at the right hand of the throne of God.

Through God's word we understand that routinely caving into sin, is never acceptable, and is never the way to deal with sin arising out of the flesh-it must be put to death by continual rejection of it when it arises, and refusal to practice it with patience and the help of the Lord. God's way is the only right way and the only right way is God's way.

The Confession Of Sin
After Salvation

This second confession (G1843 exhomologeo) commanded by God regarding sin is solely limited to relationship between believers. Believers are to mutually confess sin, for the healing/recovery and turning away from it. Also believers are to forgive one another even as Christ has forgiven them. We even forgive our enemies: Mt. 5:44.

The scriptures commands us that we should confess (G1843) exomologeo—to acknowledge or by implication of assent) agree fully:—confess, profess, our faults one to another, and pray for one another that in doing so we may be healed.

Jas. 5:15 Confess your faults one to another, and pray one for another, that ye may be healed. The effectual fervent prayer of a righteous man availeth much.

This (G1873) confession is used in the sole context in which Christians confess to one another, in mutuality for the purpose of overcoming some particular sin, and never (G3470) confession for Salvation or further forgiveness from God.

Brotherly restoration takes place amongst God's people is necessary and to be done in a spirit of meekness:

Gal. 6:1 Brethren, if a man be overtaken in a fault, ye which are spiritual, restore such an one in the spirit of meekness; considering thyself, lest thou also be tempted. So we can freely see from God's word, the ingredients of true helping in this matter, self-examination and meekness in confrontation for restoring another in the spirit of meekness, and learning to avoid this same temptation, having seen its bad effect on another.

Jhn.14: 23 Jesus answered and said unto him, If a man love me, he will keep my words: and my Father will love him, and we will come unto him, and make our abode with him. 24 He that loveth me not keepeth not my sayings: and the word which ye hear is not mine, but the Father's which sent me. God is love, and the truth is that He has given us His love, and enabled us to love Him and all men. God accepts nothing from us not given out of love. The reason that Christians obey God is out of love for Him and what He has done for them.

God is Sovereign over His people. For the protection and wellbeing of his children He exercises control over them. Out of love He will not allow his children to do things or live in ways that will harm them, and even entice others by their bad example.

God teaches, trains, helps, corrects, disciplines and sets firm/clear eternal standards for acceptable behavior and life style for His children. He has eternally set firm boundaries for what is right and good, and demands and enables His children to adhere to them. He gave us the Bible which explicitly expresses His will for us for all time. He makes it easy for his kids to please him and understand what is required of them. Rebellion or disobedience is never an option.

As our Everlasting Father, He commands relationship and obedience with Him based on love and biblical truth, not ritual based on merely keeping rules out of fear of punishment. The New Testament gives God's complete and comprehensive commands as to how the whole church must deal with sin. Beloveds we must get the fact that we cannot negotiate, or compromise with the flesh or the old nature in any way shape or form—it must be crucified: Gal 5:22—But the fruit of the Spirit is love, joy, peace, longsuffering, gentleness, goodness, faith, 23 Meekness, temperance: against such there is no law.24 And they that are Christ's have crucified the flesh with the affections and lusts. 25 If we live in the Spirit, let us also walk in the Spirit.

His standards are perfect, and His motives are always founded on His perfect, sovereign love; for His glory and our good.

Heb. 6 For whom the Lord loveth he chasteneth, and scourgeth every son whom he receiveth.7 If ye endure chastening, God dealeth with you as with sons; for what son is he whom the father chasteneth not? 8 But if ye be without chastisement, whereof all are partakers, then are ye bastards, and not sons.

In relationship to God who owns us, He commands that we repent of our sins, out of love to show our love for Him, with the knowledge that we are eternally forgiven, and our Father keeps no record of our sins. He still allows for our sin to have consequences. He will allow our rightfully suffering the consequences of sin to thwart us from continuing in ways that displease Him.

In relation to God Christians have the right, privilege, power, and command to repent of wrong doing without the slightest fear of losing

God's forgiveness. Repentance *does not mean* a loss of salvation, or forgiveness and fellowship with God. Repentance is not condemnation; it is not merely feeling sorry for our sins, but gladly turning away from them rather than practicing them. In relation to God, it is the evidence of the indwelling Holy Spirit that we obey and agree with God out of love for Him, to see sin as totally out of line with holiness.

Repentance is never passive in merely just recognizing sin. It wholly works by involving and bringing the whole of our hearts, minds and bodies in action and grateful cooperation with and to the will of God and not our own. We put it into practice in our everyday lives and interactions. This is done by the empowerment of God and in love, gratitude, thankfulness, and obedience for what God has done for us. Our growth is not static but increases through obedience, and living by God's standards.

1 Pe. 4:1-3 1 Forasmuch then as Christ hath suffered for us in the flesh, arm yourselves likewise with the same mind: for he that hath suffered in the flesh hath ceased from sin; 2 That he no longer should live the rest of his time in the flesh to the lusts of men, but to the will of God. 3 For the time past of our life may suffice us to have wrought the will of the Gentiles, when we walked in lasciviousness, lusts, excess of wine, revellings, banquetings, and abominable idolatries:

The doctrine of Jesus Christ thoroughly convinces the Christian that the practice of sin is absolutely forbidden.

God commands discipline and consistent right living in the body of Christ. The whole church has authority from God to admonish and correct one another. No one is above church discipline, which is done in love and can restore or remove as warranted. There are various ways that discipline or correction takes place in the body:

A. Conviction of our redeemed conscience by God leads us to examine and correct ourselves.
B. Authority from God to admonish one another
C. Expulsion from the church by overseers and even the body as a whole for those who refuse to repent.
D. Those who refuse are not to be considered an enemy, but can return and be received as a brother or sister again in love, if truly repentant, in word and deed. In essence discipline or correction is restorative in nature, and disciplinary in action. However, it can permanently remove people who reject sound church discipline and doctrine. The church is never to allow unrepentant sinners who reject church discipline and doctrine to remain amongst the body to tempt others to sin and bring blame upon the gospel of Jesus Christ.

THE IMPERATIVE
OF THE NEW COVENANT

We arrive at the book of John understanding its context within the frame work of the New Covenant of Grace, and not the Old Covenant of the Law. The New Covenant thoroughly debunks the error that after salvation anyone can keep coming to Christ over and over again to get forgiven for sins solely by their repetitious confessions. Christ's offering of Himself once, is sufficient and eternally effective to take away all sins and to gain permanent forgiveness for all who confess and believe on Him.

Hbr 9:24 For Christ is not entered into the holy places made with hands, [which are] the figures of the true; but into heaven itself, now to appear in the presence of God for us: 25 Nor yet that he should offer himself often, as the high priest entereth into the holy place every year with blood of others; 26 For then must he often have suffered since the foundation of the world: but now <u>once</u> in the end of the world hath he appeared to put away sin by the sacrifice of himself. 27 And as it is appointed unto men once to die, but after this the judgment: 28 So Christ was <u>once</u> offered to bear the sins of many; and unto them that look for him shall he appear the second time without sin unto salvation.

We also arrive at the book of John with the understanding that the Old Covenant of the Law and the New Covenant are two separate Covenants; that have similarities, but are extremely different from one another. The New Covenant is not an extension of the Old Covenant of the Law; it is exactly what God declares it to be-a new covenant. Most importantly we arrive with the understanding that the New Covenant is the final, finished, everlasting, incorruptible, inerrant completion of the Bible for all time. While the whole of scripture remains relevant for God's purpose; the foundation and inerrant truth of the New Covenant forms the core of Christian faith and eternal salvation. Without faith in and acceptance of the New Covenant of Jesus Christ, no one can be considered a Christian. Our understanding of the New Covenant keeps us from doing what God forbids: comingling the two covenants, and/or trying to substitute the Old Covenant of the Law for the New Covenant of Grace.

In the book of 1 John 1:1-3, the apostle presents in meticulous detail, one could even say in minutiae, the foundation of our fellowship with God and one another, God being the sole authority of which this fellowship can be made or validated.

John gives an eye witness account, up close and personal of the reality that Jesus was, seen, heard, felt, and witnessed by the apostles as well as other saints. Jesus Christ is the everlasting, eternal, preexistent God, who was revealed to them in the person of God the Son.

John wants all of God's People to know that God is not some kindly person, who saves us and leaves us alone to our own devices, sink or swim, win or lose. No, no, and no. John declares God's purpose is that we are to have what God wants-commands, eternal unbroken fellowship with God and one another—and this is according to God's eternal standard alone.

Fellowship: meaning G2842 koinōnia; *partnership*, i.e. (literal) *participation*, or (social) *intercourse*, or (pecuniary) *benefaction*:—(to) communicate (-ation), communion, (contri-) distribution, fellowship).

<u>John 1: 4 And these things write we unto you, that your joy may be full.</u>

John clearly emphasizes that God's people would understand, and know God with such infallible certainty that each and every one would be filled fully of cheerful calmness, great joy and delight.

As we rest in God in believing the eternal truth of John's message we find that our joy is full too. Dearly beloveds, we arrive at the book of John knowing with certainty that there is no expiration date on the forgiveness of our sins obtained through the final finished atoning sacrifice of our Messiah, Saviour, Redeemer, Deliverer, High Priest and Mediator of the New Covenant Jesus Christ.

There is no darkness in God whatsoever, and John is bold and explicit in stating this absolute fact:

1 John 1:5 this then is the message which we have heard of him, and declare unto you, that God is light, and in him is no darkness at all. 6 If we say that we have fellowship with him, and walk in darkness, we lie, and do not the truth: 7 But if we walk in the light, as he is in the light, we have fellowship one with another, and the blood of Jesus Christ his Son cleanseth us from <u>all sin</u>.

John's message plainly declares that just saying we are saved doesn't cut it. All who believe must also (do the word), i.e. walk in the light-in word and deed, out of love for God and others, for God enables His people to will and to do.

Easy believe-ism is out of the question here because John tells us plainly without exception, if *anyone says*, "I am a child of God; I am walking in the light, *just because I say so*. My word alone is good enough to make it so, even if I choose to walk in darkness", such a person is walking in darkness, self-deceived and deliberately trying to deceive others.

Those alone who say, believe and obey God, 1 John 1:7 tells us the blood of Jesus Christ cleanses from all sin. note all sin. These alone have eternal, unbroken fellowship with God.

John unequivocally states those words, deeds, practices in minute detail that God has set as the absolute standard that qualifies for walking in the light.

We cannot fail to understand from verse 1 John 1: 7 that it is not necessary for Christ to keep offering His blood over and over again seeing that His one-time sinless atoning sacrifice has eternally met all of God's requirements to take away all sins forever and bestow permanent forgiveness to all who confess and believe Him. Christ has achieved permanent forgiveness to all who believe on Him.

John is quite bold to declare that for believers the blood of Jesus Christ cleans them from all sin. All means in the whole, entirely, without exception.

Does God say His kids are in and out of the light; in and out of darkness; broken fellowship, quasi-fellowship, partial fellowship?

No—absolutely no. Other books of scripture backs up and agrees with the book of John:

Eph. 5: 8 For ye <u>were</u> sometimes darkness, but <u>now</u> *are ye* light in the Lord: walk as children of light: 9 (For the fruit of the Spirit *is* in all goodness and righteousness and truth;) 10 Proving what is acceptable unto the Lord. 11 And have no fellowship with the unfruitful works of darkness, but rather reprove them.

1 Thess. 5:5 Ye are <u>all</u> the children of light, and the children of the day: we are <u>not of the night, nor of darkness.</u>

The word "no" here and also in John's passages means the Greek word Ou G3756, a primary word, meaning the absolute negative.

God has no hybrid saints or in-between; half-light, half dark or sometimes dark and sometimes light children. Those in God are light, those not in God are dark, without exception.

Jesus is the perfect Saviour; there is no sin of any kind in Him. Jesus came to take away the sins of everyone who believes in His name. Not some sins, but <u>all</u> sins for <u>all</u> time.

1 John 3: 5And ye know that he was manifested to take away our sins; and in him is no sin.

John attests that anyone claiming to never having any sin at all is self-deceived, and totally devoid of truth:

1John 1:8 If we say that we have no sin, we deceive ourselves, and the truth is not in us.

What John is declaring here is that there are those who falsely claim that they have no need of a Saviour because they absolutely never had any sin. This cannot possibly be true since we know that Jesus Christ is the only sinless human being that ever lived, who came to take away the sins of the world. Again except for Jesus Christ all men are born sinners: Rom. 3:23 For all have sinned, and come short of the glory of God . . .

Now some might think that John was only addressing some folks called "Gnostics", who contradicted God's message. The Gnostics, it is said, did not believe in sin or that Christ's death was necessary for salvation. This is an extremely narrow understanding of John's passage and is actually in error of it. This highlights the problem of trying to authenticate the Gospel, by comingling it with history derived from non-biblical sources. Christians must check all teachings against scripture, without exception.

God's word authenticates God's word alone. God's word confirms, interprets, clarifies, and backs up God's word.

John speaks clearly in biblical absolutes, without apology. It is clear that John is not writing about just one certain kind of group of so called "Gnostics", he is writing in absolute terms. All persons except for Jesus Christ who claim they have absolutely never had any sin, therefore having no need for a Saviour is lying. Most profoundly, such persons are self-deceived and absolutely have no truth in them at all.

John keeps repeating and expounding on His message, he states explicitly that the Gospel is the non-negotiable, incorruptible, uncompromising, final, finished, eternal absolute standard, and unchanging truth without exception.

The Dangers of Wrongly placing 1 John 1:9 Under The Law

All attempts to place or understand 1 John 1:9 under the context of the Old Covenant of the Law always results in error that turns people back to the Law. Those who do so, in error, still acknowledge themselves as sinners, who must continually offer the confession of their sins and beg Jesus Christ to shed His sinless one time blood sacrifice to gain forgiveness for them over and over again. Instead of the fellowship and full joy promised by 1John 1:4, they are plunged into a false gospel, a toxic message of deadly deception. Having placed themselves under relentless bad news; they experience: works for rest, condemnation instead of joy, and in misery they are saved but never safe, washed, but never cleansed.

Blindly, such persons pray to an obscure false saviour of their own imagination, from whom forgiveness of sin is won and lost with no hope to attainment of permanency. Such persons continually moan, wring their hands, scream how utterly unworthy they are, beg, cry, sob, and crawl towards an imaginary false altar continually, with various sins to lie upon it. Living in abject shame, condemnation and misery of their own incorrect understanding, they continually offer up their own ineffectual offerings of "confessions" to get forgiven of their sins over and over again, through a false saviour of their own imaginings and not the true.

They experience a short lived comfort-until the next sin, to begin the unending cycle of horrific futility over and over again. Such persons cannot know the joy of full assurance declared by John.

This turns people back to the Old Covenant of the Law and away from the New Covenant of Grace. It also shows a horrific and complete lack of understanding of both the Old Covenant of the Law and the New Covenant of Grace as well, since it is clear that in both Covenants confession alone is never accepted; as God absolutely commands that it must be accompanied by an unblemished blood sacrifice of atonement administered through the high priest/mediator. Even more horrific is the failure to recognize and accept the superiority of the atoning sacrifice of Jesus Christ which does insult and despite to the Lord Jesus Christ, whose sinless blood washes every believer from <u>all</u> their sins and gives them permanent forgiveness for ever. The everlasting truth is that the superior perfect sacrifice of our High Priest,/Mediator Jesus Christ has cancelled out and replaced the Old Covenant of the Law and its priesthood for all eternity by God the Father.

The plain truth is that all believers in relation to God receive permanent forgiveness of all sins forever through the perfect sinless atoning sacrifice of Jesus Christ once for all, under the New Covenant. It is impossible for God to take away the forgiveness He has given us through His Son.

The New Covenant declares that teaching Christians to live by the Law for righteousness is turning aside from the gospel truth and teaching empty babbling, by those who neither understand nor know what they teach.

Christianity is not a religion it is a personal eternal, unbroken relationship between all believers and God. Beloveds there are no exceptions to the absolute Gospel, for those who believe incorrectly that Christians are still under the law in any way, the scriptures clearly states that God no longer accepts this way to be righteous anymore.

Praise be to God, Christ has absolutely obtained complete forgiveness from God for of all our sins forever.

John states absolutely to those to whom He has written:

1 John 2:12 I write unto you, little children, because your sins are forgiven you for his name's sake.

Salvation is the *free gift* of Jesus Christ by the grace of God to all who believe. As for those who insist on the error of the practice of continually giving their confession to God to be forgiven of sins and restore a so-called broken fellowship with God over and over after salvation; John states unequivocally: 1 John 3:4 Whosoever committeth sin transgresseth also the law: for sin is the transgression of the law. 5 And ye know that he was manifested to take away our sins; and in him is no sin. 6 Whosoever abideth in him sinneth not: whosoever sinneth hath not seen him, neither known him. 7 Little children, let no man deceive you: he that doeth righteousness is righteous, even as he is righteous. 8 He that committeth sin is of the devil; for the devil sinneth from the beginning. For this purpose the Son of God was manifested, that he might destroy the works of the devil. 9 Whosoever is born of God doth not commit sin; for his seed remaineth in him: and he cannot sin, because he is born of God. 10 In this the children of God are manifest, and the children of the devil: whosoever doeth not righteousness is not of God, neither he that loveth not his brother.

John, minces no words, leaves no room for misinterpretation. He completely destroys the error of the Christian still being identified as a "sinner" and/or "saved sinner", continually needing to beg over and over for further forgiveness after receiving salvation.

How much clearer can the New Covenant Gospel message be than that God's Son Jesus Christ's atoning sacrifice permanently gains God's forgiveness for all time and forever takes away all sins of those who believe? If anyone believes the incorrect teaching, that the relationship of God with His people can be broken, and restored over and over again by confession of human effort, and that God's forgiveness is incomplete, I pray that they will quickly repent and come believing what God tells us of Christ's work: "It is finished".

Now there is no way we can fail to understand from both the Old and New Covenants that God absolutely commands unblemished blood sacrifice to atone for sin and gain forgiveness from God see Heb. 9:22-28.

The whole of the New Covenant rules out totally that 1 John 1:9 commands that Christians keep coming to G3470 homologeo confess sin to God over and over again as though His forgiveness is temporary. Why? Christ's superior, supreme sacrifice is the completion of God's plan for totally taking away all sin, and to gain eternal forgiveness to those who come to Him by faith in His Son Lord Jesus Christ.

THE FULL JOY OF 1 JOHN 1:9 UNDER THE NEW COVENANT

In light of the New Testament of Lord Jesus Christ through whom we have received the complete atonement and permanent eternal forgiveness the sole correct interpretation 1John 1:9 can only be read as a statement of permanent eternal accomplished fact, according to the New Covenant and <u>never</u> a conditional statement as found in the Old Covenant of the Law.

1 John 1:9 If we confess our sins, he is faithful and just to forgive us *our* sins, and to cleanse us from <u>all</u> unrighteousness.

For every believer, this means that you can greatly rejoice because the forgiveness of all your sins through Jesus Christ have no expiration date of any kind it is absolutely permanently secured and obtained through God's Son forever. Therefore 1 John 1:9 is a confirmation of what Jesus Christ has already done for those who believe on Him.

1Jhn. 1:10 If we say that we have not sinned, we make him a liar, and his word is not in us.

Back in verse 1 Jhn. 1:8 we noted the false declaration of those claiming to absolutely never having had any sin. In 1 Jhn. 1:10 we note the false declaration of those who claim that they have absolutely never committed any act of sin; John declares that all such persons are liars.

Beloveds this verse confirms that other than our sinless Messiah and Saviour Lord Jesus Christ, if anybody else claims or believes that they have absolutely never even committed any sin they are only hoodwinking themselves, being devoid of the truth. Furthermore they are calling Jesus a liar, which absolutely confirms that His word is not in them at all. Other than Jesus Christ all have sinned and come short of the glory of God. Christ came to save sinners in the whole world.

Christian Identity

Jesus Christ is the source and root of Christian identity. In relationship to God, all believers are forever cleansed of all sin and forgiven <u>once and for all time</u>; under the High Priesthood/Mediator Lord Jesus Christ, our Messiah, Saviour, Redeemer, and Deliverer: 1 Pe. 2:9 But ye *are* a chosen generation, a royal priesthood, an holy nation, a peculiar people; that ye should shew forth the praises of him who hath called you out of darkness into his marvellous light: 10 Which in time past *were* not a people, but *are* now the people of God: which had not obtained mercy, but now have obtained mercy.

5 Ye also, as lively stones, are built up a spiritual house, an holy priesthood, to offer up spiritual sacrifices, acceptable to God by Jesus Christ.

What kind of spiritual sacrifices does our Lord enable us to offer up that He accepts?

Ro. 12:1 I beseech you therefore, brethren, by the mercies of God, that ye present your bodies a living sacrifice, holy, acceptable unto God, *which is* your reasonable service. 2 And be not conformed to this world: but be ye transformed by the renewing of your mind, that ye may prove what *is* that good, and acceptable, and perfect, will of God.

As priests under the High Priesthood of Lord Jesus Christ, we joyfully and gratefully give our lives as a living sacrifice out of love and trust to God who has made us His children; this is our reasonable service.

It must be without question that in Christ, all believers are equal, although some have greater responsibilities. Those that hold an office of leadership, or any office, must do so as servant leaders never as Lords, seeing we have but One Lord, one faith and one baptism.

Christians rejoice because there is no need to continually struggle to get God to forgive them over and over again, seeing that God's Son Jesus Christ has obtained permanent forgiveness for us that never is nor can be lost or diminished in any way.

The joyous saint, instead of insulting King Jesus by denying the power of His blood which gains eternal forgiveness that never is lost nor diminished after salvation; instead counts on the power of our Lord to practice a steady resistance to self and sin to serve Him our great High Priest/Mediator and Shepherd over the house of God, going from victory to victory by God's power. Repentance of sin for the forgiven saint is on-going; however the issue of God's forgiveness via atonement through Jesus is Once and for all settled for all eternity-it is finished. Jesus gave His people a new name, saints, children of light, children of the day, and many other terms of endearments out of His love for us.

We do not allow anyone or anything to change the name that our God gave us out of His love for us. God has forever settled our identity as His people, and our eternal destiny, in Him alone.

Gal. 2:20 I am crucified with Christ, nevertheless I live; yet not I, but Christ liveth in me; and the life which I now live in the flesh I live by the faith of the Son of God, who loved me, and gave himself for me. If our Lord has so loved us, dear saints, we can truly rest and trust in His finished work, that only He could do for us.

1John 2:2 And he is the propitiation (means G2434 Hilasmos atonement, I.e. (concr.) an expiator:—propitiation.) for our sins; and not for ours only, but also for the sins of the whole world.

We are given the privilege, opportunity, and commandment to repent, because we have power over sin through Jesus. We also have the command, privilege and blessing to take the Gospel message to a fallen world, and to demonstrate it in our everyday lives consistently, because we have power over sin.

Phl 4:4 Rejoice in the Lord alway: and again I say, Rejoice. 5 Let your moderation be known unto all men. The Lord is at hand. 6 Be careful for nothing; but in every thing by prayer and supplication with thanksgiving let your requests be made known unto God. 7 And the peace of God, which passeth all understanding, shall keep your hearts and minds through Christ Jesus. 8 Finally, brethren, whatsoever things are true, whatsoever things are honest, whatsoever things are just, whatsoever things are pure, whatsoever things are lovely, whatsoever things are of good report; if there be any virtue, and if there be any praise, think on these things.

Christians no longer have to beg God for forgiveness. Christians deal with sin God's way. As Christians we thank God that He will never take His forgiveness from us or allow it to diminish to us in any way. As Christians fully understand that because of Jesus Christ we are no longer under the Law, and therefore sin is neither imputed nor any record kept of them anymore. Therefore Christians gratefully repent of sin, in full agreement with God that all sin is wrong, and the only right way is God's way and God's way is the only right way. When Christians are aware of any sin in their lives they refuse to practice it in any way no matter the cost, by the power of God and out of love and obedience to Him. Christians lead a life of believing God and living out His word in public and in private. Christians rest in complete faith in the final, finished, inerrant, incorruptible, uncompromising, and complete work of Jesus Christ. Because of Jesus we are no longer servants of sin, but joyful servants of righteousness.

Every Christian can joy richly in the full assurance of the eternal love and forgiveness of God that has absolutely no expiration date, because of what Lord Jesus Christ has done for us.